DESERT ROSE

The Search for My Lost Lesbian Aunt

LYNN ROMAINE

DEDICATION

Dedicated to all beings and creatures
made less in the world by
what we say about them,
especially to
my Aunt Rose,
who was born a hundred
and eighteen years ago.

CONTENTS

ACKNOWLEDGMENTS

RESEARCH

Cindy Hayostek, Douglas, AZ Historian

Lyn Killian, San Bernardino Historical and Pioneer Society

PHOTO RESTORATION

Thank you, Asia Harman. Great job!

KICKSTARTER

Sylvia Atkinson

and

K.M. Kaze

for

Making significant Kickstarter donations

Which make this book possible.

1 PREFACE

This book is dedicated to my Great-Aunt Rose, whom I never knew, but whose life has become more remarkable as society moves to accept the differences in people. This book is an unraveling mystery, compiled from the few official records of Rose I discovered digging around online, the limited number of photos from my dad, and preciously few family anecdotes about Rose's life. The rest of the material I discovered traveling west on a forty-day odyssey, tracking down the family tale that Rose had died in an Arizona insane asylum years before I was born. Anyone who knew or cared about what really happened to Rose was dead, more than twenty years. That left it up to me to gather together those bits and pieces of evidence I have and retell the story of Rose.

The Turner Family

Back Row: Julia, Effie, Carvel, Myrtle

Front Row: John, James (father), Altha, Narcisa (mother), Rose

2 ROSE'S FAMILY TREE

Rose's Parents

James L. Turner (1840-1918)

Narcisa Davis Turner (1868-1902)

Rose's Siblings

*Effie F. Turner Murrill (1881-1957)

—Married Fred A. Murrill

—Son, Glenwood Clark Murrill (1911-1999)

—Granddaughter, Judi L. Murrill Romaine (1944-)

*Myrtle L. Turner Calvird (1883-1920)

—Married to Charles Calvird (1883-1933)

*Carvel Turner (1884-1956)

*John S. Turner (1887-1959)

*Jane Altha Turner Hovis (1889-1971)

*Julia Turner Morris (1892-1979)

*Rose Clara Turner (1896-1970)

*Siblings of Rose

3 INTRODUCTION

My Great-Aunt Rose is a mystery to me. I never met her and what I did know about her came from offhanded remarks and faded photos passed down by my father and his family. Whispered, casual descriptions like 'strange' and 'different' and even 'crazy,' followed any mention made of Rose. When I got old enough to ask where Rose lived, my grandmother or her sisters would answer, "Rose went crazy and died a long time ago in an insane asylum in Arizona."

It was easy enough to realize that Rose was the embarrassment of the family and would receive nothing more than an asterisk in the Turner family story. Once I grew up I realized all the secrecy surrounding Rose was because she was a lesbian. She dressed in men's clothes and made no attempt to behave feminine.

My Dad, Rose and Effie

While no one ever mentioned her sexual preference, I always knew as a child that she was not an acceptable female. Living in the early twentieth century this behavior was especially taboo. And that was the astounding thing about Aunt Rose; she was born in the Midwest at a time and a place with strict views on gender roles. It was clear from family anecdotes and photos that she ignored those Victorian conventions. Instead she had chosen a path for herself that was remarkable.

Over a century after Rose was born, I had decided it was time to go on a quest to find the real Rose. As I dug deeper into her life, I discovered I was inspired not only by Rose's audacity, but by the possibility that every marginalized person can live courageously. This book is in honor of Rose, real person, with the same joys and struggles we all confront.

4 WHY AM I WRITING THIS BOOK?

That young child who was curious about Rose grew up and forgot all about her, the lost little sister of the Turner family. I went about my own life, getting married, having a home, a career, and a child. Then, nineteen years ago the story of Rose resurfaced. I was fifty-five and in college. It was during a class in semiotics (the study of signs and symbols) that I remembered Rose, and I decided to write a paper about the meaning of her life. I interviewed my 84-year old dad, who was a nephew to Rose, and he gave me what he could of his wispy memories. I unearthed all of the family photo albums and found eight or ten photos he identified as Rose. I researched the meaning of cross-dressing in the early twentieth century, and wrote a ten-page academic paper on the interpretation given Rose by her family and by society. I then promptly forgot about her again, except for a few genealogy searches out of curiosity over the next fifteen years.

Then two years ago, as I was closing in on seventy, I found myself in a position to sell my house, buy a trailer, and take to the road. My dream was to see America and complete whatever was incomplete in my life at that point. While arranging my travel plans, I found Rose repeatedly cropping up in my thoughts. So I combined my desire to relive my hippie days through a great road trip along with a cross-country search for Rose. The last known contact she made with her sisters from Arizona or California was in the late 1920's. My plan was to visit Arizona and find out if she really did die there in that 'insane asylum.' I would search whatever hospital records I could find; city and state directories; track down if possible where she had lived; how long she had lived; and discover what sort of a life she had led. And I wanted to find her grave.

5 FACTS ABOUT ROSE

Rose Clara Turner was born in 1896 in St. Francois County, Missouri, the youngest of seven children. Originally from Clay County, Tennessee, her father, James L. and mother, Narcisa (Nancy Davis) Turner, moved to St. Francois County sometime between 1884 and 1887. They settled in lead mining country, sixty-five miles south of St. Louis. The family was made up of two boys and five girls: Effie (my grandmother) was the oldest, born in 1881; Myrtle was born in 1883; then Carvel, born in 1884; John, born in 1887; Jane Altha, born in 1889; Julia, born in 1892; and Rose. The family was left motherless in 1902 when Narcisa died of tuberculosis.

Source: A 1902 obituary for Narcisa (Nancy) Davis Turner in Deslodge, St. Francois County, Missouri, which mentioned leaving behind a husband and seven children.

Source: Three census reports—1900, 1910, and 1920, that included Rose Turner.

The 1900 Census listed Rose as Clara, her middle name, age four years.

The 1910 Census, which I recently discovered, listed Rose as Rosa, age 14, living in a household in Idaho Springs, Colorado, with her oldest sister and my grandmother, Effie, now married to Fred Murrill. Also listed were her sisters, Julia Turner, age 18, and Jane Altha Turner, age 21, with her husband. All were reported residing in Idaho Springs Ward 2, Clear Creek, Colorado, which is 32 miles west of Denver.

The third and last census record I found for Rose was 1920, where she was listed as 20 years of age (actual age was approximately 24), a boarder, yet again, in the household of Effie Turner Murrill and Fred Murrill in River Rouge, Michigan. Effie was once more running a boarding house, this time down river in Detroit. Living there along with Rose was my dad, Glenwood Murrill, age 8, the only child of Effie and Fred; Rachael Murrill, age 20, also listed as a boarder; and two other boarders. Rachael was a first cousin to Fred Murrill and not related to Rose. She was to play a role in Rose's life in the future.

Source: Death records and obituaries

I found the death record for James L. Turner, who died in 1918. I also found the death certificate and obituary for Myrtle, who died in Cochise County, Arizona in 1920.

I found no census records for Rose Turner beyond the 1920 census.

Source: Multiple photos of Rose identified by my dad before he died.

6 STORIES ABOUT ROSE

I continued to consider Rose's story without doing further research for eighteen years. It was those pictures that sparked my real interest and I began to study them, pondering Rose's life. The photos of Rose and her friends were so intriguing I kept imagining their world in the late 1920's and how their lives had played out. What most captured my attention in all the photos were the happy faces, so unlike other photos of my dad's family, showing dour, serious people, looking like they had little to smile about. Rose's friends looked like they were playing dress up. This seemed to contradict the sad story of poor, crazy Rose.

Before I headed off on my quest, this is what I knew about the family based on stories and suppositions.

The Family Narratives

Let's start at the beginning with the Turner family, ten or more years before Rose was born. Between 1884, when the first son, Carvel, had been born, and 1887, when the second son, John, was born, the family moved from Tennessee to St. Francois County, Missouri. The only industry in that part of Missouri was lead mining. Hearing stories from my grandmother and my dad that mining was the occupation of the county, I surmised that James Turner had moved his family to find work in the Missouri mines.

They arrived with three children—Effie, Myrtle, and Carvel. In the next fifteen years they had four more children—John, Jane Altha, Julia, and Rose. The family photo shows two adults and seven children looking well dressed and well fed.

My grandmother had two stories she told about her family. First, when her mother contracted tuberculosis and died in 1902, my grandmother was left to care for the six other children. She complained a great deal about having to take on the role of mother at the age of 21. She didn't mention what the income source was for the family, other than her husband working at a tool and die job in the mines.

The other story my grandmother loved telling was that her father was an alcoholic, who died in a barroom brawl, stabbed in the eye, over another man's wife. *Ugh.*

My grandmother never mentioned the specifics of raising the younger children except to bluster that she'd been forced to take on that role. She often talked about her sister, Myrtle, who died of consumption in in 1920 in Cochise County, Arizona. The story she told was that Myrtle and her husband, Charlie G. Calvird, moved to Arizona around 1918 to get work. She combined these facts with a wild, colorful tale of Myrtle being bitten on the breast by a rattlesnake, inferring that she died that way, forcing my grandmother to raise Myrtle's son Everett, along with my dad. Everett was known to be a homosexual throughout his life from high school on and died in 2011 at the age of 95.

While Myrtle moved with her husband to Arizona, my grandmother never mentioned Rose moving there or ever visiting Myrtle. It's unlikely that Rose followed Myrtle to Arizona in 1918, since in the 1920 census; Rose was listed as a boarder in my grandmother's house in Michigan.

My grandparents and my great aunt Altha with her husband, moved to Michigan from Colorado around 1911, where my dad was born. I could only surmise that from 1911 up to the 1920 census, Rose was living with Effie in Detroit, or with her sister Julia in Missouri.

I have a few postcards written in 1918 and 1919 from Myrtle's husband, Charlie, to my grandmother, where in one instance he asks how Rose is doing living with Julia, who by 1918 was married and living in Deslodge, Missouri. Where Rose was between the 1920 census and the last photos inscribed with California, 1928, is unclear.

New Power Plant (Copper Queen).   BISBEE, Arizona.

Queen Mine postcard from Charlie, Bisbee 1918

I asked my dad questions about Rose a few years before he died in 1999. At that point he was into his 80's and Alzheimer's had begun to have an affect on his memory. That, and the passage of time, made his stories vague. He did recall Rachel Murrill, who boarded along with Rose, as someone very pretty who he assumed was a barber since she cut his hair. He also remembered that Rachael and Rose left together in a car heading west. He talked a lot about Rose's gun and holster that he wore in the picture with Rose and his mother. He looked about ten years of age, which would place that photo around 1920.

My Dad with Rose's gun and holster

My Dad did not remember seeing Rose again after she left with Rachel, but mentioned that when he knew her she always wore men's clothes and that she was nice to him and. In my last interviews with my dad, he could not help adding that she was 'that way,' meaning lesbian.

Rose and Rachel

A major barrier to thinking there might have been something more to Rose's life was my grandmother's repeated account that Rose died a long time ago. With no more information or mention of her beyond 1928, the conclusion I came to was that she died in the late 1920's or early 1930's.

What Else I Surmised From The Stories, Photos, And Facts

From the photos I knew there that there was enough money for Rose to leave Michigan in a car. I had three photos of cars; two with 1928 Arizona license plates, with the words 'California desert 1928' scrawled on the back and the third one a different model.

Rose and her friends were dressed strikingly well compared to the pictures I had of other family members in the 1920's. I knew Rose took her gun along, which seemed useful for women traveling in the West.

Rachel, a Friend and Rose

In studying the photo of the entire Turner family (see Rose's Family Tree), it struck me that Rose was the only one who looked normal.

Here is a brief retelling of the Turner saga of death and violence:

Myrtle died in her early thirties (1920) of TB, as had the mother of the family in her late thirties; James, the father, died in a barroom brawl; Jane Altha, became a family legend, reportedly sleeping around with men, including her husband's brother. Then there was Julia, the sweetest of the children whose life was filled with misery—her husband committed suicide in his mid-thirties; her oldest son, Tom, murdered his twenty-four year old wife, Audrey, in a fit of jealousy and then turned the gun on himself, leaving his daughter Patty orphaned. Of Myrtle's three sons, the youngest, Everett, was raised by my grandmother, who made repeated attempts to 'cure' Everett of his homosexual tendencies. And then there was Patty, Julia's only grandchild, who died at 25 of unknown causes; and finally, my older sister Gay, who died at 17 in a violent car crash. Through all this my grandmother ruled over the remaining members as though a queen. Not the happiest of families.

So before I set off to find the story of Rose, I could not help but believe that with all the unhappy family history, Rose had made the best of things for herself by heading west. I was hopeful.

7 THE TRIP WEST

I left on my road trip with plans to do research in Arizona, where Rose was last known to have been and to get a book into print with her photos by 2014.

In preparation I used Ancestry.com and other online search engines to gather additional material about Rose and the Turner family.

That done, I headed west in late September of 2013. (*See my two small e-books, published exclusively in Amazon Kindle Store, about my odyssey on the road.*)

My first layover was in the San Francisco Bay Area where I had ten days of housesitting, free from other demands, where I began to write the book. While staying in the Bay Area, I made a visit to the Gay and Lesbian Center at the San Francisco Public Library. While they were interested in my project, they had only local databases and archives, searchable by name, dating back to the 1960's. After two hours of aimless searches I left, having hit the first of many dead ends. At that point, aside from one photo of Rose marked 'California desert 1928,' I had no evidence that she had ever lived in California.

At the end of my stay in San Francisco, I headed southwest toward Arizona to search through state historical records. At that point, I was hopeful I would find documentation of Rose living there, as well as evidence she *had* or *had not* been institutionalized there. I had thoroughly searched Ancestry and found no death certificates for a Rose Turner who died in Arizona fitting my Rose. So my only pieces of evidence of an Arizona connection were the picture of her and her friends sitting on a 1928 Buick with the Cochise County license plate; the family story that Rose died there; and the knowledge that her sister, Myrtle, had died in Bisbee in 1920.

8 SEARCHING FOR ROSE

After idling my way through Nevada and Utah into Arizona, camping and enjoying the beauty of the desert, I eventually landed at Kartchner State Park, midway between Tucson and Bisbee, where I planned to stay while I did my week of Rose research.

On the first day, I left my trailer at the state park and drove the hundred miles west, heading for the Arizona History Museum and Library in Tucson. Those first three hours of searching city directories for Bisbee and all the online databases for Arizona genealogy were bewildering. When I found nothing, I had no idea where next to look. I did begin to understand that, as in my California research, unless a person came from a settler or very early Arizona name, there would be no record of that person. Historic records for ordinary people were almost impossible to come by.

About to give up on the History Library, I caught the attention of a new employee who got interested in my story. It was then I began to realize that finding research partners along the way, people with some interest in the story of Rose, would make all the difference in finding any information. The employee and an intern dug around with me and together we found the Bisbee newspaper microfilm files from 1920. With the date of Myrtle's death in mind from Ancestry, I found Myrtle's four-line obituary. It was astounding how exciting it was to find even one tiny reference to the family, as if it somehow made the entire search valid in that the Turner family did exist.

While Myrtle's death notice included only a few lines, it contained basic facts that were crucial to narrowing down my search and eliminating suppositions. The newspaper stated that Myrtle had lived in Bisbee and even gave her address, which eliminated my need to search further in Douglas, another thirty miles away.

Charlie and Myrtle

The article gave no next of kin except her husband, Charles Calvird. The small obituary also said Myrtle's body was being shipped back to her home in Deslodge, Missouri that same day, where she would be buried. In doing a brief search of her husband on Ancestry, I traced him back to Missouri as well, where he lived out the rest of his life, remarried with children. With that, I knew that when Myrtle died in 1920, the ties to the Turner family and Arizona had been severed. This small piece of information narrowed down my need to search in depth for further records of Rose tied to Myrtle in Bisbee, although I still had the mystery of Rose sitting on the 1928 Buick.

To be thorough I decided to go to Bisbee and once more search the local city directories, along with tax and business records to see if I could find any trace of Rose having lived in Cochise County, Arizona within the ten years leading up to her 1928 photo.

While in Tucson I followed up on two other suggestions from the History Library. Wingspan, the Antiviolence Gay and Lesbian Center of Tucson, turned out to have tiny offices set back in an obscure strip mall on a crowded street in a low-income section of the city. The organization was made up of sweet, young people, who seemed to be desperate to look tough. They did express an interest in my Aunt Rose's story but they had no historic resources or databases available to them that might be useful.

From there I searched out a tiny University of Arizona Gay, Lesbian, Bisexual, Transgender (GLBT) office again hidden away, but this time in a two-story apartment complex on a busy street. It took persistence to get into the building and find the place. As it turned out, the office was opening that week and the director was a graduate of Indiana University in Bloomington, Indiana. She told me the disappointing news that they had no records earlier than the mid-twentieth century and very few of those, at that. She had no other ideas.

I left Tucson dispirited and at a loss as to what to do next but was relieved to drive the two hours back to my trailer sitting beneath Kartchner Cavern Mountain. As it turned out, the next day a sandstorm took out ninety cars on that same stretch of I-10 I'd driven to and from Tucson, so something good had come of my going when I did.

After seeing the most extraordinary sunset (see the cover of my last book, *Wander)*, the next day I left my trailer behind again and headed for Bisbee. With the sunset of the night before, I had a strange sense of Rose and Myrtle accompanying me as I drove the eighty miles to Bisbee. I had little to distract me from the barren beauty of the land on the empty two-lane road and had plenty of time to imagine Rose driving along, laughing with her friends in her 1928 Buick.

Bisbee turned out to be a charming, well-preserved mining town that had experienced a boom in the late nineteenth and early twentieth centuries. Built on the back side of rugged mountains with a tunnel for access to the town on the other side, Bisbee sat on top of the largest of three mines that had turned it into a thriving community for many years. I pulled up a steep drive to a parking lot that turned out to be the tour office for the Queen Mine, the largest and only mine still with a presence in Bisbee. These days the mine was merely a historic site with hourly tours available underground. When I arrived, a tour group was getting suited up in hard hats and raingear. I asked questions of the history ladies at a little information table at the start of the tour and they pointed me to the tour guide, a young, personable man. I specifically wanted to know about Myrtle's husband, Charlie Calvird, and whether there were any records I could see of past employees to verify that Charlie had worked at Queen Mine. I was hoping for dates of employment to confirm that he left his job when Myrtle died in 1920. The tour manager told me that, unfortunately, the mine had destroyed all the employment records twenty years ago, fearful of class action law suits from families of men who died working in the mines. The tour guide told me that copper was the main ore of Queen Mine, although they did mine for lead as well. This fit perfectly with Charlie and Myrtle having moved from Leadwood, Missouri, a lead mining area, to Arizona. I also discovered that in 1917 there was a major strike of the miner's union and a thousand miners were 'deported' from the mine, historically called the Bisbee Deportation. With that, a thousand miners were brought in from other states to take the jobs of those union workers—another explanation of why Charlie and Myrtle with their three boys had moved to Bisbee. The tour guide pointed me to the Bisbee Historic Center where his sister was the head of archives.

I then moved on to the Historic Center where I spent an entertaining two hours talking with volunteers. They did their best to fill me in on whatever they could find, which was mostly city directories. I went through them once more very thoroughly with no results for Myrtle, Charlie, or Rose. I also browsed the old books on the mines but found nothing I could use and left with a promise that the archivist would be at work the next day and might have additional records in her collection.

I drove slowly back to my trailer, having failed again. By now I was starting to realize that historic research could be a tedious, head-butting grind, mostly turning up little usable information.

I returned to Bisbee the following day where the archivist was able to copy the funeral home records of Myrtle's death. This record had no more information about other family members at her funeral and again I was left at a dead end.

I stayed one more night at Kartchner. In the morning, I hooked up my trailer and began the 1600-mile journey back to Indiana. I was determined to stop for a few hours in Douglas to be sure there were no records of Rose, Myrtle, or Charlie in the county records building. I spent two hours there with a volunteer but after searching all records of home ownership, businesses, tax records, and any auto purchases for the years 1918 through 1928, I had no results.

Next I hit the local Douglas Buick car dealership, around since 1910, the oldest in Arizona. The manager could only verify that the car Rose and her friend sat on was a 1928 Buick and it probably had been purchased in Douglas since the license said Cochise County, Arizona.

Rose and her Friend and the Buick

My last activity in Douglas was to head for the local history museum and that is where my fortunes changed. An interested and helpful woman who worked as a researcher sat with me for over an hour as I related Rose's story and the research I had so far. She told me she had access to the local hospital and institutional records and would make a thorough search the next day, looking for any records of a Rose Turner having been incarcerated or having died in Arizona. She promised me that if the records were not there, it was close to impossible that Rose had been institutionalized or died in Arizona, as the state kept excellent records.

From there I headed for home, angling northeast on Arizona 80 out of Douglas. The next day as I camped in northern New Mexico, I got the e-mail from my Douglas researcher that there were *No* records of a Rose Turner in any of the historic data. I felt immense relief that now I could rule out the family legend—Rose did not die in an asylum in Arizona, nor was she ever incarcerated in a hospital or asylum there.

As I drove toward Indiana the next three days, I continued to be in e-mail contact with my Douglas historian and she repeatedly urged me to get a copy of all possible death certificates for Rose Turner, whether it seemed likely or not it was *my* Rose. A year before, I had found a death certificate for a Rose Turner who died in California but I had been so sure Rose had died in Arizona, I had adamantly ruled out the California Rose, especially since she died in 1970, many years after my Rose was said to have died.

9 BACK HOME IN INDIANA

I arrived back in Bloomington on November 5th, having driven forty days and 4,500 miles. With my Douglas historian still insisting I get that death certificate, I immediately put in an order for it from California, costing me $41 that I felt was a waste of money. The only good I could see coming from this action would be to rule out that Rose Turner.

Four days later I got the death certificate in the mail from the State of California. I read through it tentatively at first, then with growing excitement reread it, as it became clearer that this could possibly be my Rose. The birthdate was within four years of what I had obtained for Rose on Ancestry, and the death certificate listed Missouri as her birthplace, also right. Her parents were listed as unknown, which was disappointing, *but* it did state under spouse '*Never married.*' That fact alone raised my pulse and I began to believe this could be my Rose Turner. The other piece of extraordinary information on the death certificate was the listing of the exact date and place of death: San Bernardino County, California, and under 'how many years residing in the state,' it read '30 years.' The death certificate also said Rose Turner died in the Highland Nursing Home where she had resided for six months. Finally, the certificate listed employment as 'owning gas stations.'

Now I had Rose's place of death, date of death, name of nursing home, cemetery where she was buried, and even what type of work she did. But I still had no hard proof with next of kin to absolutely confirm this was my Rose Turner. In the end the most important piece of information was the name of the person responsible, Lucy *Smith*, who lived at the same address as Rose. At last I had a name of a person connected to her.

Sitting out the winter in Indiana, I began an exhaustive four-month search to either accept the death certificate as Rose's or to rule it out. I needed to find a reference to Rose's next of kin or I needed to find relatives of the Lucy *Smith* who had been responsible for Rose to see if they could give me more information.

Once I had the date of death for Rose, I spent hours doing searches on Ancestry but nothing new turned up. I then went about searching for her housemate on Ancestry. Within a matter of hours, I found Lucy *Smith* along with her place of burial and date of death. This confirmed for me that Lucy had been buried in the same cemetery as Rose. Most important, I found Lucy's family members on Ancestry who had done their own family trees including Lucy. I proceeded to e-mail the families who gave Lucy *Smith* as an ancestor, asking them for any information on Rose.

Within a few days I received an e-mail from one family member who said they knew nothing about Rose, but a brother-in-law knew something.

Next came one of the biggest surprises of my search and a very surreal experience. I got a call from a man identifying himself as the grandson of Lucy *Smith*. He introduced himself, and said, *"Yes, I knew Rose."* !!! He told me he was young at the time and was only twenty when Rose died, but he remembered her well. He had a lot to say about his grandmother divorcing her husband, meeting Rose, and that Rose and Lucy had been housemates for many years until Rose died in 1970. He gave me information about their work and that they had met in a café and gas station in Desert Center, California, where they both waitressed. He also mentioned that he thought together they had run a café and gas station. He explained that his grandmother had worked at Patton Hospital in San Bernardino for many years as a nurse. He also remembered his grandmother talking about Rose's gun, although he had never seen it.

At this point, I was close to declaring this was my Rose. More important, I was excited and happy to think that Rose had not lived and died alone; and in fact, had lived into her seventies.

I next contacted the mortuary but was told they kept no old records. I then called the Montecito cemetery and they confirmed they did have a record of Rose Turner being buried there. What was exciting was that Lucy was buried in the same cemetery. The cemetery people told me they would go out to Rose's plot and get a photo of her headstone and grave. But the cemetery e-mailed me a few hours later saying that her grave was unmarked. It was a very sad moment. Lucy had her stone, probably purchased by her family, and Rose had none.

From that point, I spent the next two months sure this was my Rose Turner, but I still wanted absolute confirmation.

My Researcher

Weeks passed as I sat out the coldest, snowiest winter in Midwest memory with nothing new coming along; no useful social security records, nothing in the California Archives, or the California History Museum. All attempts to find confirmation of Rose's work or taxes she paid failed. What I needed was Rose's obituary, if there was one.

I made numerous calls to the San Bernardino Library and the librarian told me they could not search their microfilm for an obituary. I then contacted the San Bernardino Historical and Pioneering Society. Within a few weeks and many more calls, I was connected to Lyn Killian, who proved to be an invaluable research partner. She agreed to search the library microfilm for Rose's obituary. She also agreed to make a visit to Patton Hospital to see if she could get access to employee records as I had begun to think perhaps Rose had worked at Patton as well as Lucy, and that they had met there. Underlying this focus on Patton Hospital was a fear that Rose could have been a patient there, something I dreaded, since Patton was a mental hospital. If she had been a patient, that information would put me back to the original family narrative.

But two weeks later I got great news! It's astounding how searching is so similar to being in a room pushing at the walls and suddenly a door appears. My researcher had found Rose's obituary and she read it to me over the phone: In it was absolute proof that this was my family's Rose Turner, as it listed her living sisters, Julia and Altha, as her next of kin. This was the proof I'd been waiting for!

Further Research On Patton

I was getting closer to the finish line for Rose's story when I again began to have my doubts about where Rose had ever been a patient at Patton Hospital and again speculated that Lucy and Rose could have met there. I was suddenly back in the childhood tale that Rose had been institutionalized at Patton, a hospital for the criminally insane, in particular because Rose had preferred dressing as a man which in those days could have been considered grounds for imprisonment. And if so, I wondered if Rose was released into the care of Lucy as her custodian. Or was it simply that Rose's housemate worked at Patton and nothing more? With those fears resurfacing, I turned, to my local library to check databases for Patton Hospital. We found the 1930 and 1940 census with lists of all patients incarcerated during those years and there was no Rose Turner in either census. *Relief.*

But I still needed to get a clearer picture of the Patton Hospital connection and so I sent another e-mail to Lucy's grandson.

2ND Call From Lucy's Grandson

Lucy's grandson called me immediately and told me the following: There was no Patton Hospital connection between Rose and Lucy as far as he knew. He again stated that Rose and Lucy met as waitresses at Desert Center Café before Lucy worked at Patton. He told me that he never knew a time when Rose and Lucy were not friends and living together, which was at least as early as 1951. He gave me the following further history, as he knew it: Lucy retired from Patton Hospital sometime in the later 1950's. Regarding Rose's mental health, he recalled no conversation ever referring to Rose as someone unstable or with any sort of mental issue. He also mentioned that his grandmother worked on a ward with violent men, that she was very small but tough, and that she would keep them all in line. Lucy and her husband had divorced before he was born and he never knew his grandparents when they were married.

10 ONE MONTH UNTIL PUBLICATION

March was now upon me and with the April 1st, deadline for the Kickstarter book looming six weeks out, I needed to write with an eye to completing the project. But more material began showing up as my San Bernardino County historian continued pursuing various leads. I did continue digging for more Desert Center information. I talked with the chamber head of the tiny town of less than 200, to the grandson of the founder of the town and to two delightful ranchers who knew as much about Desert Center as anyone. But no one remembered Rose or Lucy.

My historian also sent me photos of Rose's gravesite without a headstone.

Rose's gravesite marked by an empty space and tree branch

The historian also found a few articles in a local newspaper mentioning Lucy *Smith* and she also sent me Lucy's obituary, which gave no mention of Rose. Even with more information out there, I needed to leave that for future research and write the book with what I had. I'd spent hours and hours of the four months since returning from my trip contacting the California Archives, the California History Society, the California State Library, the San Bernardino History Society, the car museum in Flint, Michigan, with many more hours spent at my local genealogy library using their databases. I had put in calls to the Kinsey Institute and even the Indiana University Government Publication Library with more questions about finding lost family members. Many of the hours spent went nowhere, but the tiny gems of information that turned out to be true gave me so much more about Rose's life than I ever could have imagined at the start of this project.

11 THE FINAL STORY – FOR NOW

Here is my story of Rose's life for now, including all the facts I have and all the suppositions I freely make here.

Rose Turner was born in the lead mine country of Missouri into a family who moved there from the hill country of Tennessee. She was born in 1896, the youngest of seven children, five girls and two boys. They were a family who struggled but were not desperately poor, having enough money to clothe the children well and even take photographs. The father was a miner while the mother was a homemaker. When Rose was four years of age she lost her mother to TB and from that point until adulthood, she lived with various older sisters.

Around 1909 when Rose was thirteen, she moved with three of sisters to the mining town of Idaho Springs, twenty miles outside of Denver, where her sister, Effie, ran a boarding house. During those years in Colorado, Effie ran the Murrill House while her husband worked in the nearby mines.

The Murrill House in Idaho Springs

In 1911 the sisters and their families left Colorado and moved to Detroit where the men found work in the salt mines. From then on it was likely that Rose lived mostly with her sister, Effie, often traveling back and forth to Missouri where she lived with her sister, Julia, now married herself to a miner. It is possible that Rose may have even gone all the way to Arizona sometime during those years from 1917 to 1920 to visit her sister, Myrtle, in Bisbee. But most of Rose's growing up years were spent in Missouri or Michigan. In the year 1918, when Rose was twenty-one, her father was murdered in Missouri but all indications are that Rose had never lived with her father after her mother's death.

The big life event for Rose came sometime in the 1920's when she left Detroit with her car, her six-shooter strapped to her hip, and two friends. She headed west with two female friends, including Rachel Murrill, a cousin of Fred Murrill. What happened in the next years is still a mystery, only hinted at in the photos she sent back. These all showed women in the desert, often sitting on a car. In every photo Rose was smiling or laughing, looking nothing like her dour sisters still living in the Midwest.

Rachel, Rose and a Friend in the California Desert

From that point on through the 1940's, those twenty to twenty-five years of Rose's life are still missing. The good news is that the family story was wrong. Rose did not die in an Arizona insane asylum, but died many years later in 1970.

So where was Rose during those missing years? I can only imagine her moving from place to place in the West, doing odd jobs, working at gas stations or cafes, having the time of her life.

Then in the early 1950's there she is working in that quirky little town in the Mojave Desert called Desert Center, she meets Lucy *Smith*, a divorced mother of three with grandchildren who works at the café as a waitress.

Desert Center Café and Gas Station

Some time in the next year or two, Rose and Lucy decide to share a house in San Bernardino County, a hundred miles to the west.

During the next twenty years, with Rose and Lucy living together in Lucy's house, they buy a gas station or even more than one with Lucy herself continuing to work as a nurse at nearby Patton Hospital. They settle down and for many years live a happy American life in that little house.

Then in early 1970, Rose, who is fourteen years older than Lucy, becomes ill enough that she is admitted to Highland Nursing Home, where six months later she dies of congestive heart failure and diabetes. Her attendant at her death is Lucy. I imagine the sadness Lucy must feel in losing her long-time companion, Rose, who is buried in nearby Montecito Cemetery. Twenty-four years later Lucy dies and her grandchildren bury her there as well.

So that is Rose's story for now. I took a few liberties and added some things I could only assume yet I can't help but believing that Rose lived a full and happy life.

12 WHAT'S NEXT?

I am not done with this book. I am still determined to find those missing 1928 and 1950. And I intend to search out neighbors and friends still alive who knew Rose and Lucy in San Bernardino County. And I want to fill in specific questions not yet answered:

—Where did Rose get the money to live for those fifty years after she left her family?

—Did the 1928 Buick belong to Rose? If so, where did she get the money to buy such a fancy new car?

—What happened to Rose's traveling partner, Rachel Murrill? Did she come home, leaving Rose out west, to eventually marry and settle down herself?

—What about those gas stations owned by Rose? Where were they and did she really own them?

13 WHAT DID I LEARN?

I learned that the stories told about us after we are gone make our lives what they were. Along with the memories we leave behind, it is the stories that continue to live on after us. I learned that Rose was an adventurer who found a way to live true to her self long before the time when women were free to follow their own paths. For me, Rose represents all people who have felt that they do not belong, but who have the courage find a place for themselves.

Finally, with the sales from this book I intend to buy Rose Turner a headstone that will rewrite her story. It will read something like this:

Rose Turner, 1896-1970—a woman who

lived boldly and went before many to follow

ABOUT THE AUTHOR

Lynn (Judi) Romaine grew up in Detroit, Michigan surrounded by the various great aunts and uncles mentioned in this book. While straight herself, she was married for twenty-five years to a gay man and together they had a gay daughter who is happily married, living in Seattle. Judi feels that Rose's family story made her own life richer and gave her a unique path to follow. The retelling of Rose's story is a completion of her commitment hat every person matters, whatever the choices or circumstances.

www.ingramcontent.com/pod-product-compliance
Lightning Source LLC
Chambersburg PA
CBHW050832290526
45792CB00001B/359